Swan Song

A play

Vanessa Brooks

Samuel French—London
New York-Toronto-Hollywood

SWAN SONG

The first version was produced at Jill Freud's summer theatre season at Southwold in August 2000. This version was produced at the Trinity Arts Theatre, Tunbridge Wells in April 2002 with the following cast:

Margaret	Alwynne Taylor
Donald	Michael Elliot
Mimi	Joan Blackham

Directed by Vanessa Brooks

CHARACTERS

Margaret, hardworking, caring, Donald's unmarried secretary; 50s-60s
Donald, sardonic and weary Chartered Surveyor; 50s-60s
Mimi, Donald's wife, a lonely lady of leisure drowning in luxury, boredom and alcohol; 50s-60s

SYNOPSIS OF SCENES

The action takes place in Donald's office on the first floor of Sykes, Austin and Didcott-Price, a long established firm of small town surveyors

Time—the present

SWAN SONG

Scene 1

Donald's office on the first floor of Sykes, Austin and Didcott-Price, a long established firm of small town surveyors. April. 9.00 a.m.

A large desk dominates the office. On it sit a document tray, blotting pad, telephone, desk lamp and various bits of paraphernalia. Opposite this desk there is a smaller desk on which sit a typewriter, notepads, calendar and telephone. A kettle, two teacups and saucers and two plates are on a table in the corner. There is a hatstand by the door which leads out to further offices and the stairs down to the ground floor. A window, covered by a blind, offers a view down to the High Street and across the road to the cinema. A large mirror hangs above a fireplace which is supposed to be in the fourth wall

Music

Margaret enters in a raincoat, carrying a damp umbrella and a cake box. She places the cake box on the small table. She takes off her coat and hangs it on the hatstand along with her umbrella. She walks to the "mirror" and tidies her hair. She walks to the blind and opens it slightly before sitting behind her desk. She takes the cover from the typewriter and finds a half-completed letter. She feeds the sheet of A4 into the machine

Donald enters, also wearing a raincoat. He carries a briefcase and umbrella. Donald and Margaret exchange the briefest of nods. Donald looks in the "mirror", combs his hair and straightens his tie. He crosses to the blind and rolls it up completely before crossing to the tea table and looking inside the cake box. Margaret re-arranges the blind to her liking and sits again. She types. Donald leans over Margaret's shoulder as she types until she is intimidated into stopping and Donald crosses to his desk

The music fades out

Margaret continues to type until she becomes aware of Donald watching her. Her typing grinds to a halt

Margaret Is something wrong?
Donald What?
Margaret Mr Sykes?
Donald Um?
Margaret I said, is something the matter?
Donald Yes. I've got nothing to do.
Margaret Oh dear.
Donald Help me, Margaret. Give me some meaning on this my final day.
Margaret This needs your signature.
Donald My signature?
Margaret Please. Twice if you can manage it.

Donald crosses to Margaret

Donald So it's come to this.
Margaret There.
Donald Thirty-five years of sweated labour.
Margaret And there.
Donald Endless study of the finer points of surveydom.
Margaret Thank you.
Donald To scrawl my name across a piece of paper. I seem to remember that's how it all started. Drawing pictures of houses in red crayon. Have I come full circle? Will I regress, Margaret? Will early retirement lead me inevitably back into nappies and liquid food?
Margaret We said we wouldn't be maudlin, didn't we, Mr Sykes.

Donald Did we.

Margaret Yes we did. We whispered our agreement over any other business in yesterday's board meeting.

Donald Must have been asleep.

Margaret Mr Sykes …

Donald There's only so long you can listen to a youth with spots droning on about new technology before your eyes mist over and your brain atrophies. They should hang a sign over the front door. "Sykes, Austin and Didcott-Price, Citadel to the triumph of youth over experience".

Margaret Every dog has his day.

Donald crosses to the "mirror" and examines himself

Donald And even young dogs have worms. Do I look old, Margaret?

Margaret Compared to who?

Donald Terence Stamp.

Margaret He's immortal. Eternally beautiful.

Donald All right. Kirk Douglas.

Margaret Plastic surgery queers the pitch.

Donald Sir John Mills?

Margaret A spring chicken by comparison.

Donald Do I look sick?

Margaret No more than usual. I saw you at the doctor's last night. Twice in one week. A record even for you.

Donald I didn't see you.

Margaret Mother parked the electric wheelchair behind the rubber plant and I was partially obscured by her rain canopy. I could see you but you couldn't see me.

Donald Must give MI5 a call. They'll put the flags out when they know you're available for work.

Margaret You looked anxious.

Donald I've been having the pains again. Only worse. Much worse in fact.

Margaret That is a worry.

Donald Not for Mimi. She's delighted. Her smile broadens in direct correlation to my every twinge. As if there's an invisible string between my tightening arteries and the corners of her mouth.

Margaret That's a terrible thing to say.

Donald It's true. She wants me to keel over and release the insurance money.

Margaret Don't be absurd.

Donald They only stump up if I drop dead in harness. She's got eight more hours. She'll be at home now sticking pins into a wax effigy praying for me to slump over the desk by five o'clock.

Margaret That's wicked.

Donald That's my wife.

Margaret What utter rubbish. She's concerned about your health. I know she is.

Donald Only because it may affect her plans for the high life on the Spanish Riviera. Illness clouds the sangria and taints the shrimp. Angina lowers the tone in Fuengirola.

Margaret I had no idea the tone there was that high. In fact I didn't think there was much of a tone at all. Well is there?

Donald It's your stunning insight that's kept me going all these years. That and your apple doughnuts.

Donald heads towards the tea table. Margaret steers him away

Margaret Agenda and correspondence before cake. As ever.

Donald Today is exceptional — let's indulge in brazen anarchy and imbibe sugar before eleven o'clock.

Margaret It's routine, structure and schedule that keeps everything ticking along. You'll realize that once you're retired. Mother lives by the clock. Or at least she used to. When she knew what a clock was. She put it in the oven yesterday and gave the lasagne pride of place on the mantelpiece.

Donald What would she do without you? You're a marvel.

Margaret All I do is keep her in line.

Donald I wish I had you to keep me in line.

Margaret What do you mean?

Donald You'd do it so gently and so tactfully I'd hardly realize I was being straightened out. You treat me like a peony in a pot that must be encouraged to flourish. You are my Alan Titchmarsh. You tweak and nurture. Mimi is my Slobodan Milosovic. I'll be razed to the ground within a week. I'm terrified, Margaret. I've spent most of my married life avoiding my wife. From tomorrow all of that changes. We have to actually be together. Every day. We don't even have any kids to take the pressure off and a dog's out of the question as we're emigrating. Well, supposed to be … I was rather hoping you'd … Save me.

A silence

Margaret What?

Donald So what's on the agenda today, Miss Pitts? How many nibbles of bricks and mortar have you prepared for me to feast upon?

Margaret Mr Kingston of the shopping centre project has scheduled a phone call to you.

Donald When?

Margaret Nine thirty this morning.

Donald The man is an unmitigated bastard.

Margaret Urgent he said.

Donald An urgent bastard. Even worse. Chrome stairways and chrome lifts designed by a man with chrome spectacle rims and a chrome soul. "Great Chromium" that's what they'll rename these islands in a few years time. The rest of the world will be wearing dark glasses to shield themselves from the glare of our artificiality.

Margaret He needs to talk to you about the specs for the architraves on top of the pillars at the drive-through McDonald's.

Donald And I need to talk to him about art, culture and an architect's responsibility. Shall we engage an interpreter?

Margaret And I've scheduled a call for you ——

Donald Make it a good one. A humdinger for my final day.

Margaret — with Simon Fox at Donaldson and Dicks. He phoned three times yesterday. Come four o'clock he lowered himself to faxing Melanie a photocopy of his bottom.

Donald Raised himself. Do you know he threw fourteen people
with learning disabilities out of their homes in order to build his
fitness centre? Just how healthy can *that* be?

Margaret We are instructed by him. We've yet to send the final
survey. It's right here. Shall I post it?

Donald Don't know. Feels like sending a map of Poland to Hitler.
What else do I have to look forward to during these my dying
hours?

Margaret Messrs Austin Price, Samuels, Davies, Smith and
Campbell would like to make a presentation to you at three
o'clock in the boardroom.

Donald That's much more like it. How much was in the kitty, Mata
Hari?

Margaret Melanie sacrificed her bingo money and the partners
were very generous. Well, most of them.

Donald I bet Samuels didn't put his hand in his pocket. His wife's
probably sewn them up after his affair. He practically bankrupted
himself. He was travelling to Derby three times a week. She was
a stable girl. He nearly got away with it until Jean found a load of
sugar lumps in his Y-fronts. You can't deceive a wife forever, can
you? Best to be honest. Up front. In matters of the heart.

Margaret I wouldn't know.

Donald What about Campbell? Ready to fill my shoes, isn't he? I
caught him in here the other morning with a paint shop colour card
miming handshakes. As for Austin Price he's so gaga he probably
put a groat in the collection envelope. So come on, what am I
getting?

Margaret I'm not saying.

Donald A Teasmade?

Margaret Stop it.

Donald Golf clubs? Silver mug? Tie clip?

Margaret Mr Sykes.

Donald A gilt framed photocopy of all of their ——

Donald } (*together*) { — arses.
Margaret }   { That is enough. People have raised money
                              and are giving you …

Donald Yes?

Margaret What they're giving you out of the kindness of their hearts.
Donald Really?
Margaret There is good in the world if you care to look.
Donald I do. And I see you.

A silence

Margaret Mr Sykes …
Donald How's your mother?
Margaret My mother?
Donald The doctor's. Last night.
Margaret Oh fine. She's fine.
Donald That's good. That she's not entirely dependent on you. Because I was ——

The phone rings. Margaret crosses to her desk and picks it up

Margaret (*on the phone*) Mr Sykes' office. … What? … Melanie, take the gum out of your mouth — you sound like a herd of elephants marching through mud. … Just a moment. (*Holding the phone to her chest*) It's your wife.
Donald All right.
Margaret (*on the phone*) Put her through.

Donald picks up the phone on his desk

Donald (*on the phone*) Mimi. … Yes. … Yes. … What?… No. … Because … *No*, Mimi — Hallo?… Hallo… (*He puts the phone down*) Damn … Damn … *Damnit!*
Margaret What on earth is the matter?
Donald I … *Damn.* I'm sorry.
Margaret That's all right I ——
Donald Shouting like a fool, it's just I … She's coming in at lunchtime … I had my own plans. My own plans for today. I wanted to what I want to do. It's my last day, damnit.

Margaret You were going to the pond.

Donald I've never mentioned ——

Margaret I know that it's a special place for you. I've seen you nip into the baker's for bread and once — years ago — I … followed you. Now there's a confession for *my* last day.

Donald When?

Margaret The end of my first week here. I'd picked up my wage packet from Mr Austin-Price. 1964 — so it must have been eighteen pounds, five shillings and sixpence. I had my sandwiches in my bag and I thought I'd sit by the pond for half an hour. I was surprised to see you there. You seemed too grown up for that sort of thing.

Donald Twenty-three, man of the world.

Margaret I thought you'd be in a pub somewhere impressing Mimi. But there you were standing by the edge of the water looking very pensive. And you walked towards the lock.

Donald Go on.

Margaret You took a bag of bread from your pocket and fed the swans. I stepped back into the bushes and suddenly you ran at them — there must have been about six or seven — you ran hard at them so that there was a sudden white eruption and they took off and flew then turned in the sky back towards us and they were making the most incredible sound with their wings. Like …

Donald Like an orchestra of cellos.

Margaret Yes, an incredible humming. And these giant beautiful birds filled up the sky and I looked down for a second into your face and … Well… You … You were …

Donald Yes?

Margaret You were crying. And I felt a tenderness towards you. A … warmth.

Donald Really?

Margaret Yes. It touched me.

Donald Touched you?

Margaret Yes. Here. (*She indicates her heart*)

A silence

Donald			Margaret I…
Margaret	}	(*together*)	{ I'm sorry, that was terribly unprofessional of me.

Donald			It's all right
Margaret	}	(*together*)	{ Rude. Personal.

Donald			No. No I …
Margaret	}	(*together*)	{ We need to sort through the files I'll …

The phone rings

Donald			I'll pick it up. It's probably ——
Margaret	}	(*together*)	{ I should think that's Mr ——

Donald and Margaret reach the phone at the same time and their hands become intertwined on top of the handset. They look at each other for a moment. Margaret moves away

Margaret I'll put the kettle on.

Donald picks up the phone

Donald Donald Sykes. … Ah Mr Kingston. … No, by all means talk chrome and beef burgers at me, my secretary is about to supply me with copious amounts of coffee and selfless support— I can cope with anything that's thrown at me. With her help.

Music

Black-out

SCENE 2

The same. 11.00 a.m.

Margaret arranges teacups at the small table. Donald looks through the window

Donald Don't tell me. If I gaze at the front of the Odeon for long enough it'll come to me. The best film Oscar in nineteen sixty-four went to — *My Fair Lady*!

Margaret Yes. Of course. I went with mother on the Sunday before I started working here. I was fifteen. I remember coming out and looking up at this office window thinking I could do with a little bit of blooming luck.

Donald You didn't need luck, Margaret. You've always been a very gifted secretary.

Margaret Do you think so?

Donald I was blessed the day you walked through that door.

Margaret That's about the nicest thing anyone's ever said to me.

Donald Dreadfully slow at making tea though. How much longer for my cake? I'm starving for my elevenses.

Margaret The kettle needs to boil. We really must sort through these files.

Donald *The Sound of Music*. That was the year after, wasn't it? There was a cardboard cut-out of Julie Andrews in nun's habit standing in front of the butcher's. Remember? I came in one morning and looked down there to see her with a black pudding beard and sausage-meat where her eyes should be.

Margaret An acquired taste, Julie Andrews.

Donald Not one for butchers' boys obviously. That was the year Mimi and I got married. Funny. I recall Julie Andrews with chipolatas on her face more readily than I do my own wedding.

Margaret You were a little under the weather.

Donald Titanically hung over. I'd had a crisis just before dawn. Bill talked me out of it.

Margaret You had doubts?

Donald There was somebody else. Somebody else whose face haunted me. Whose touch I craved. Somebody else who I loved.

Margaret Poor girl.

Donald She was none the wiser.

Margaret Ignorance is bliss.

Donald You and Bill had a bit of a thing going didn't you?

Margaret We went to the pictures. Once. Saw *In the Heat of the Night*.

Donald Sydney Poitier. He had style.
Margaret Bill didn't. He was extremely fresh.
Donald You can't blame him. He'd fancied you for months.
Margaret Nonsense.
Donald Left town after the wedding. After doing his best man bit.
  Once he knew there was no more hope.
Margaret Rubbish. I'm no heartbreaker.
Donald Yes. Well. That's blissful ignorance for you, isn't it.

A silence

Donald The following year it was *Oliver!*.
Margaret No. It was *Midnight Cowboy* before *Oliver!* wasn't it?
Donald No, the next Oscar winner was *Oliver!*, then *Midnight
  Cowboy*, then *Patton* and then — *Love Story*?
Margaret Didn't win the Oscar.
Donald I'm surprised. Romance and cancer, sounds like a dead cert
  to me.
Margaret It was my favourite film. I saw it five times in total. A
  Saturday afternoon ritual of mine. Sitting alone in the dark.
  Losing myself for a bit. Hoping I suppose that I might fall in love
  and … And then Mother had her first stroke and that was the end
  of that silly nonsense. Tea's ready.
Donald Marvellous.

*Donald and Margaret sit down at their separate desks with their tea
and doughnuts. Donald eats very quickly*

Donald What will you do? Now I mean.
Margaret The cardex files need to be sorted. The drawings need
  to be boxed and labelled and the correspondence log could do
  with ——
Donald I'm talking about your life. Not the paperwork.
Margaret Oh. My life. I see.
Donald Didcott Price didn't make any offers?
Margaret With the email and the Internet they only need one
  secretary and Melanie is more than capable of walking and
  chewing gum at the same time.

Donald So you and your mother will tick along?

Margaret Yes.

Donald In the same house? Together. All day long. Until — well, I suppose, until she …

Margaret Oh gosh I'm sorry. I'm so sorry. (*She bursts into tears, crosses to her bag and finds a paper tissue*)

Donald Here. Take mine. It's clean. I think. I'm so sorry. How crass of me. Wittering on. Is she really very poorly?

Margaret What?

Donald Your mother? I presume the doctor had some ——

Margaret I just feel a little overwhelmed today. It's been thirty-six years. Thirty-six years that we've worked together in this office and I know, I just know, that I will miss it terribly. Won't you?

Donald Yes. But more than that, much more that that I'll —— (*He suddenly cringes with pain and clutches his chest*)

Margaret Mr Sykes?

Donald Pills. Where are my pills? I …

Donald finds his pills in his drawer, Margaret rushes for water from the small table

Bloody childproof lid. Need to be Charles Atlas to get the thing off. Oh damn it …

Donald spills tablets on the floor, Margaret helps him to pick them up

Margaret } (*together*) { Here let me…
Donald   { All over the shop ...

Donald I'm falling apart.

Margaret You ate your doughnut too quickly. Maybe you are regressing. If you carry on bolting your food like this Mimi will have to wind you after every meal.

Donald She winds me before every meal and at regular intervals throughout the day. With words like a fist to the solar plexus.

Donald and Margaret knock their heads together

Margaret ⎫ (*together*) ⎰ Ouch.
Donald ⎭   ⎱ Ouch.

Margaret laughs, as does Donald as he helps her to her feet

Donald What? What are you laughing at?

Margaret Me sobbing, you with chronic indigestion and a box full of files here that we've spent the past two hours avoiding. Small wonder that they're putting us out to grass.

Donald Speak for yourself Miss Pitts. Let's go to work. Three piles. For upstairs. For Melanie. For the bin. Agreed?

Margaret Agreed. Here. The Donaldson and Dicks file. It's time for your scheduled call to Simon Fox.

Donald Let's get it over with then. Light touch paper and stand clear. Number.

Donald takes the file and picks up the telephone. Margaret opens the file

Margaret (*reading*) Zero-seven-four-two-nine, three-one-zero, eight-five-three.

Donald dials

Donald Hello ...

Margaret Extension two-oh-five.

Donald Extension two-oh-five please.

Margaret Be careful, Mr Sykes. They have brought a lot of money to the company over the ——

Donald Money. Pah ... Fox? Donald Sykes. ... Yes I do have the survey. ... Yes I'm sending it to you today. ... No, it was completed three weeks ago, I chose to make you wait. ... Because I despise you. ... (*With his hand over the mouthpiece, to Margaret*) I've wanted to do this to a client for thirty-six years. (*Removing* *his hand*) The house on top of which you intend to build your gym — which by the way is terribly passé and doomed to failure — houses twenty long-term residents with special needs who have no desire to be made homeless. ... I am simply saying that I cannot abide you and that I hope you live a short life in abject misery. Good-day, goodbye and good luck. You need it. (*He puts the phone down*)

Margaret Bravo.

Donald Tell Melanie to send him the survey with an invoice. And make sure that call is itemized and charge him double for it. Aside from the presentation that finishes the work for the day. Take an early lunch. I'm going to. There's something I have to do. (*He puts his raincoat on*)

Margaret Wait. Here. (*She produces a small plastic bag from her handbag*) Mother and I bought far too much bread this week.

Donald You really did know where I was going today.

Margaret I'm your secretary. I know you better than you know yourself.

Donald Come with me.

Margaret What?

Donald Come and feed the swans with me. For old time's sake. Only don't watch from the bushes, stand by my side.

Margaret But Mimi will ——

Donald Mimi will be here at one. It's just gone twelve. Let's spend an hour together. On our final day. Will you come?

Margaret Yes, Mr Sykes. I'd love to. (*She picks up her coat and puts it on*)

Donald Margaret, it's been thirty-six years. I think you've earned the right to call me Donald.

Margaret and Donald exit

Black-out

The same. 1.00 p.m.

The Lights come up on Mimi looking at herself in the "mirror"; she is stony-faced. She lights a cigarette and trembles slightly. She finds a bottle of Scotch in Donald's desk drawer and pours some into a teacup. She touches Margaret's desk and typewriter when she hears Donald and Margaret approaching and moves to the corner of the office

Donald and Margaret burst into the room

Margaret That was amazing, Donald. Truly amazing. You know so much about nature and bird life. To think I've spent all this time with you over the years and I've never really known you at all. Not properly.

Mimi Join the club.

Donald } *(together)* { Mimi. Christ.
Margaret } { Mrs Sykes. I didn't see you there.

Mimi Where have you been?

Donald We … We …

Margaret We delivered a survey to Donaldson and Dicks. It took quite a while to explain the irregularities surrounding the party wall issue.

Mimi And that was truly amazing for you? Small wonder you're still a spinster in your fifties.

Donald Mimi.

Margaret Well — well — er — I mean — I …

Mimi Nature and bird life in a business meeting? And I always laboured under the misapprehension that you worked for a living.

Margaret I'll take these files down to Melanie. Have a nice lunch.

Mimi Highly unlikely.

Donald Yes. Yes. Thank you, Margaret. Thank you.

Margaret exits

Mimi. What do you ——

Mimi Sit down.

Donald discovers the whisky bottle on top of his desk

Donald Is that my Scotch? At one o'clock in the afternoon. In a teacup.

Mimi I didn't notice any crystal.

Donald Sorry there's no bloody ice.

Mimi Oh there's plenty, Donald. You're skating on it. It's always been thin. But now it's cracking. *Will you sit down.*

Donald sits

It's quite remarkable. The ability that one can acquire to close one's eyes to the truth. To enjoy the sensation of the dark. Blissful ignorance I think it's called. I've been caressed by a lie for the past thirty-six years. It's hidden in the cashmere you bought me. The silk scarves. You've muffled my screams with soft furnishings and slowed my feet with shagpile carpet. But one can choke as readily on rose petals as on nails, my love. One can kill with kindness but you can commit bloody murder with guilt.

Donald How much have you had?

Mimi I noticed you hovering this morning. You always hover when you're up to something. Like a fly with no sense of direction. You were buzzing about in the hallway. By the postbox. "Coffee's ready," I said. Expecting you to come through to the kitchen. But instead a strange shuffle to the patio door and then "I'm off to the office," you shouted. Cheerio and you were gone. Do you know what I can't believe? The way that you've watched me night after night. Packing our suitcases. We've chatted about the journey. About the meetings Sally and Bill have lined up for us with estate agents. They expect us tomorrow afternoon, Donald. Going to meet us from the plane and take us to the villa, aren't they? But then again maybe not … (*She produces a crumpled piece of paper from her bag*)

Donald Ah.

Mimi Yes. I sat for quite a while at the breakfast table looking out at the garden. Thinking what an odd mood you'd been in these past months, putting it down to retirement blues. Then I noticed the birdbox. Have you lost your mind?

Donald Christ. Mimi let's ——

Mimi The bluetits were flying around squawking like bloody starlings. Couldn't get in to feed their babies. So I walked outside and pulled the letter from the airline out of the hole. Two air tickets cancelled a week ago. I must have startled you when I asked if you wanted coffee. When the hell were you going to tell me?

Donald Look I ——

Mimi It stopped hurting quite so much after the third vodka and orange.

Donald I just ——

Mimi I've known for years. She's been besotted with you. She goes pink whenever you're near and laughs at your morbidity. You aren't funny or interesting, Donald. It's just that she's in love with you.

Donald What? No — no that's not … I just don't want to go to …

Mimi What's the plan?

Donald I — I don't know. I haven't thought that far ahead.

Mimi She doesn't know does she? Doesn't know that you can't face coming to Spain with me because you're in ——

Mimi } (together) { — love with her.
Donald }   { Stop it. Stop it now. I just don't want to go away, I …

Mimi I love you, Donald. Always have. All these years. I love the shape of your body in the bed and the smell of your skin and I would do anything for you. Why are you doing this to me? (*She sobs*)

Donald I'm sorry. I'm sorry, I can't help it, I ——

Mimi Who is it to be? Me or her.

Donald I don't know. I just don't know.

Mimi Then you have to decide. This afternoon. I can't do it for you. I'm just going to carry on. Yes? Sun tan lotion. New luggage. And then I am going to the travel agents and booking us on to a flight to Spain tomorrow.

Donald But ——

Mimi I'll be back here at five o'clock. It's up to you.

Margaret (*off*) Mr Sykes is at lunch with his wife.

Margaret enters

Oh sorry. I had no idea you were still here.

Mimi Obviously not. There's some sort of smudge on the end of your nose. Look.

Mimi shows Margaret her face in the "mirror"

Oh silly of me. Blackheads. Make your choice, Donald.

Mimi exits

Music. Black-out

SCENE 4

The same. 3.00 p.m.

Donald paces up and down, Margaret sorts through her desk drawers

Donald Bloody Spain. Bloody wine. Bloody seafood. I'm allergic. So much as a whiff of paella I turn puce and hyperventilate. And why the rush?

Margaret She knows that if she doesn't nudge you and keep you moving in the right direction you're likely to seize up and stop altogether.

Donald You make me sound like a faulty lawnmower. I just hate feeling trapped like this. Why can't I be free? Why do I have to choose?

Margaret You mean you'd rather go somewhere else other than Spain?

Donald No — no, oh Christ, Margaret I ——

Margaret If you could go anywhere in the world. Where would it be?

Donald It'd be ... It'd be a small house in a green valley with a keep in the garden. I'd sit out there for days watching the birds, watching their wings trace patterns across the clouds as time washed the sky with different colours.

Margaret You didn't finish telling me. By the pond. The story about the swan.

Donald You don't want to hear.

Margaret Oh but I do. I really do.

Donald When I was boy. Seven or eight. I found a single swan caught up in a fishing line. On the stream near our house. I recognized him. He was part of a pair that lived on a pond in the town. They mate for life, swans, and I knew this fellow — a very distinctive black mark on his head. I bent down with my penknife and set to work.

Margaret You freed him?

Donald Yes. And then I decided to shoo him in the right direction. Back towards the town. He was weak so it took some doing to force him into flight. But eventually he skimmed the surface of the water and then with a billowing sound he took flight. I ran down the hill in the shadow of his wings. Faster and faster until ... The most awful thing. The swan flew into the electricity cables that hung from the pylon. His huge wings tip to tip conducted the current through his body and sparks flew, there was a terrible scream and he fell to the earth, dead.

Margaret And you cried. Like you were crying that first time I saw you at the pond.

Donald Wept like a baby. I'd heard a swan's song, Margaret. Not from its beak but from its wings. The most beautiful sound. The final flight towards its love. That's a swan's song. Do you understand?

Margaret Yes. Yes I think I do.

The phone rings

(*On the phone*) Yes. … Yes, I'll tell him. … Yes. (*She puts the phone down*) They're ready for you in the boardroom. All of the partners. It's time for your presentation.

Donald I wonder if I could … If we could perhaps … Perhaps after work we could have a drink. A farewell drink.

Margaret Mrs Sykes will be ——

Donald To hell with Mrs Sykes. After work. I need to talk to you.

Margaret You'd best not keep them waiting. They've woken Austin Price. You don't have long before he falls back into his afternoon coma.

Donald Please.

Donald exits

Margaret picks up the phone

Margaret (*on the phone*) An outside line, Melanie. And "What d'ya want?" is not an acceptable way to answer the telephone. … I am senior secretary until the end of — Hallo?

Margaret sighs and dials

(*On the phone*) Hallo? Mummy?…Mummy it's me. Margaret. Your daughter. … Margaret. … *Margaret.* … Mummy, listen, I'll be late home tonight. … Late home. … Tonight. Yes. … I'm going for a drink with Mr Sykes. … I know he's married. …I'm not shouting. … I'm not shouting. … *I am not shouting.* … Mummy, I'm in my fifties and I haven't had a moment's enjoyment for the past thirty years, please don't deny me this. … You'll cope. … Yes you can. … *I am going out for a drink and that is final, you silly old bag.* (*She slams the phone down then picks it up rapidly. Very quickly*) Mummy, I'm sorry I'll be home late, that's all, I love you. (*She puts the phone down*)

Donald enters looking furious. He stands with leaflets in his hand

Donald Word for Windows? Word for Windows? I'll give them a word for bloody windows. Bollocks — that's my word for windows.

Margaret I did tell them a computer was a rotten idea.

Donald I'm retiring, not going back to square one. I ask you. Once upon a time you were allowed to wear Crimplene trousers and talk drivel when you hit sixty-five. Now you're supposed to go back to college and crush your aching limbs into trendy clothes. A computer. Why not a protractor and compass?

Margaret I think they were hoping you might donate it back to the firm. They need another terminal for the temp. Here.

Margaret finds a package in her drawer and hands it to Donald

Donald What's this?

Margaret Consolation prize.

Donald I haven't bought you anything. I thought they'd be giving you something and I ——

Margaret It doesn't matter.

Donald (*opening the package*) Binoculars.

Donald goes to the window and tests the binoculars

Margaret Do you like them? The man in the shop said they're the best you can get. Perfect for birdwatching. Lightweight with a high magnification.

Donald They are superb. Superb. Take a look.

Margaret Goodness. I can see right into the cinema foyer. Those new ice creams are one pound seventy-five each.

Donald Daylight robbery.

Margaret And the butcher's. The sirloin has a bit of a green tinge today and … Oh.

Donald What?

Margaret Mrs Sykes. She's just stepped out of the travel agents. She looks very happy. She's holding something …

Donald Let me see. (*Taking the binoculars*) Airline tickets. She's done it. I don't believe it. Damn. Damn. Damn. (*He pulls the sash down on the window*)

Margaret Does this mean you're going. Tomorrow?

Donald Margaret, I have something to say. Something important. I'll — I'll miss you.

Margaret I'll miss you too …

Donald No. No hear me out. I'll miss you in a way I didn't think
I would. These past weeks have been hell. Thinking I won't see
you every day. That I won't be … Close to you any more.
Margaret … I love you …

Margaret Oh Donald.

Donald From the moment you stepped through that door all those
years ago I've been in love with you. The night before my
wedding — it was your face that tormented me. Your skin that I
longed to touch. Your hand that squeezed my heart. I ached for
you and I was so confused I just got blind drunk and went through
with the wedding anyway thinking that at least I'd be near you
every day of the week. All this time it's been you … You who I've
really loved. Say something. Please. Put me out of my misery.

Margaret I …

Donald Yes?

Margaret I love you too.

*Margaret steps towards Donald and kisses him cautiously. She
steps back*

Donald Oh Margaret. What now?

Black-out

SCENE 5

The same. 4.45 p.m.

*Margaret and Donald pack separate cardboard boxes on the top of
their desks with great urgency*

Donald A boiled egg. Usually. Two slices of toast thickly buttered
and several cups of coffee. How about you?

Margaret Muesli. And Earl Grey.

Donald I have quite a routine on Sundays. Newspapers in bed and a walk in the afternoon.

Margaret Oh me too. I mean the walk. Not the … Is this your hole puncher or mine?

Donald It's ours.

Margaret Yes I suppose it is. We — we could travel perhaps. See the country.

Donald See the world. As long as we steer clear of Spain. Margaret, you are sure? Sure about the feelings that you have for me?

Margaret I've never been more sure about anything in my entire life. I've cared for you, very deeply, for the past thirty-six years. This is the perfect ending. I'm absolutely sure. (*She crosses to Donald*)

Donald Five fifteen. We'll meet at five fifteen in the foyer of the cinema, next to the kiosk over there — yes?

Margaret How will you tell her?

Donald I'll call her tonight from the hotel. Tell her to go ahead on her own. She'll have Sally and Bill to curse me to. What about your mother?

Margaret She already knows I'll be late. I'll call the agency nurses tonight. I have money put aside. It will be costly but at least it means whatever time we have left we can have together.

Donald Time we have left? You make us sound like a pair of geriatrics.

Margaret Neither of us is young and ——

Donald You make me feel young.

Margaret But you have your heart problem and ——

Donald No. You listen to me. Our time together is not going to be about illness, Margaret. Hospitals, doctors and pills. I couldn't bear that. I really couldn't bear it.

Margaret Couldn't you?

Donald We have the moors to explore and the skies to watch. I want you fit and healthy, do you hear me?

The phone rings. Margaret picks it up. Donald puts on his coat

Margaret *(on the phone)* Hallo. … Yes, I'll tell him. (*She puts the phone down*) Mr Austin-Price would like to say his final farewell.
Donald Two meetings in one afternoon. He'll need a week off to recover.
Margaret Hurry — before he fires you.
Donald Five fifteen. Outside the Odeon.
Margaret Five fifteen.

Donald and Margaret kiss

Donald exits

Margaret tidies, puts on her coat and looks at herself in the mirror. She crosses to the window and looks out. The phone rings

Margaret *(on the phone)* Hallo?… Mr Sykes is in with Mr——Who is it?… The doctor. … For me?… Just a moment. (*She sits. On the phone*) Put him through. … Hallo, Doctor. … That was quick — the marvels of modern medicine — you only did my tests last night. … An emergency?… What?… I see … No, I'm still here. … Is there any room for doubt?… No, thank you for telling me straight. … Yes, I will. … Goodbye. (*She puts the phone down and walks to the window*)

Mimi enters

Mimi Where is he?
Margaret Oh Mrs Sykes. You startled me. He was in with the Managing Director and then he was nipping out … For something.
Mimi I thought I ought to check that he had his pills.
Margaret Here. He left them here.

Margaret finds pills in the desk drawer

Mimi Just in case he has an attack on the aeroplane. It's all stress-related you know. The doctor says there's very little physically wrong with him — a few months in the sun and he'll be right as rain. Ironic really, he can't tolerate illness in others yet he's the most dreadful hypochondriac. Is everything all right with your mother?

Margaret What?

Mimi I saw you last night. Outside the doctor's. You seemed upset.

Margaret My mother is absolutely fine.

Mimi I'm glad he's shot of this office. He's come home every day with a strange smell on him. The smell of dust and decay. You've no idea where he went?

Margaret Yes. I can see him. Look. Over there. In the cinema foyer.

Mimi looks through the window

Mimi What on earth is the old fool up to? Eating popcorn like a teenager. Making an exhibition of himself. He looks like he's waiting for someone.

Margaret Yes. I wonder if you could give him a message from me.

Mimi I suppose.

Margaret Could you tell him I've enjoyed today and that it's been unlike any other day. That the possibilities were exciting and that my wings were lifted by the idea of escape. But tell him I've become caught in the cables and that today was my swan song. Not his.

Mimi Your swan song. Not his.

Margaret Please.

Mimi Goodbye then. Are you ——

Margaret Goodbye.

Mimi exits

Goodbye.

BLACK-OUT

FURNITURE AND PROPERTY LIST

SCENE 1

On stage: Large desk. *On it*: document tray containing files, blotting
pad, telephone, desk lamp, pens, etc. *In drawer*: bottle of
pills, bottle of Scotch

Small desk. *On it*: covered typewriter with half-typed letter,
notepads, calendar, telephone, pens, sheets of A4 paper,
hole-puncher. *In drawer*: gift-wrapped pair of binoculars

Table. *On it*: kettle, jar of coffee, 2 teacups and saucers, 2
plates, spoons

Hatstand

Window blind closed

Off stage: Damp umbrella, doughnuts in a cake box (**Margaret**)
Briefcase, umbrella (**Donald**)

Personal: **Margaret**: handbag containing paper tissues and small
plastic bag of bread
Donald: comb, pen

SCENE 2

Re-set: Kettle with hot water on table

SCENE 3

Personal: **Mimi**: handbag containing cigarettes and lighter, crumpled
piece of paper

SCENE 4

Off stage: Leaflets (**Donald**)

SCENE 5

Re-set: Bottle of pills in **Donald**'s desk drawer

Set: Cardboard boxes on both desks

LIGHTING PLOT

SCENE 1

To open: Full general lighting

Cue 1   **Donald**: "With her help." Music   (Page 9)
           Black-out

SCENE 2

To open: Full general lighting

Cue 2   **Margaret** and **Donald** exit   (Page 14)
           Black-out

SCENE 3

To open: General lighting

Cue 3   **Mimi** exits. Music   (Page 18)
           Black-out

SCENE 4

To open: General lighting

Cue 4   **Donald**: "What now?"   (Page 22)
           Black-out

SCENE 5

To open: General lighting

Cue 5   **Margaret**: "Goodbye."   (Page 25)
            Black-out

EFFECTS PLOT

Please read the note on page vi concerning the use of copyright music